A Date in Paris
-
The Online Dating Cleansing Program

based on the bestseller

The Four Secret Rings of

Love and Happiness

Richard Henry II Hains, CD, BAp, MSc, MBA, EMBA
Couple & Relationship Psychotherapist

A Date in Paris - The Online Dating Cleansing Program

Copyright 2017 by Richard Henry II Hains

All right reserved. No part of this book may be reproduced in any form without permission in writing from the publisher, except in the case of brief quotations embodied in critical articles or reviews.

While the author and publisher used their best efforts in preparing this book, they make no representations or warranties with respect to the accuracy or completeness of the contents of this book. The advice and strategies contained herein may not be suitable for your situation. You should consult with a professional where appropriate. Neither the author nor publisher shall be liable for any loss of profit, or any other commercial and personal damages, including but not limited to special, incidental, consequential, or other damages.

2017 edition

Library of Congress Cataloging-in-Publication Data
Richard Henry II Hains

A Date in Paris - The Online Dating Cleansing Program

ISBN-10: 0-9986806-4-8

ISBN-13: 978-0-9986806-4-4

1. Marriage 2.Communication in marriage. 3. Love. I. Title.

We hope you enjoy this book from French Amour™. Our goal is to provide high quality, thought provoking books and products that connect truth to your real needs and challenges.

A Date in Paris - The Online Dating Cleansing Program

to Henry, Rose and Andrea

A Date in Paris - The Online Dating Cleansing Program

A Date in Paris
-
The Online Dating Cleansing Program

is a trademark

Other Books by French Amour™:

The Four Secret Rings of Love and Happiness™

The Journal - The Four Secret Rings™

The Secret Art of French Love-Making™ *(coming soon)*

Golden Heart™ *(coming soon)*

Contents

Introduction.. p. 15
Discovering Your Relationship Patterns .... p. 25
The Four Secret Rings of Love and Happiness ....p. 41
The Perfect You.. p. 42
The Big WHY and S.M.A.R.T Goals........................ p. 53
The First Secret Ring: Self-Love............................... p. 71
Self-Responsibility... p. 73
Self-Affirmation...p. 79
Self-Improvement..p. 87
Self-Forgiveness..p. 97
Self-Appreciation..p. 103
The Second Secret Ring: Intimacy...........................p. 115
Emotional Intimacy..p. 115
Spiritual Intimacy...p. 123
Physical Intimacy..p. 127
The Third Secret Ring: Communication..................p. 135
The Fourth Secret Ring: Goals and Values.............p. 149
Daily Journaling..p. 161
Your Parisian Date:.. p. 253
Conclusion... p. 271

Acknowledgement

The power of God is immense and limitless. This statement is especially true with this third book, this cleansing program. Along the way, an author finds support that will help him breakthrough the wall of the "first book". It is the unconditional support and love that surrounds him that inspire the author to continue sharing its message. In this particular case, my wife is my everything. The "woman with the golden heart" was the one pushing my boundaries, my comfort zone, to help me share my message with millions of people.

Our new editor, Sheila, is also a blessing. Her professionalism, intuition, and understanding of the message behind *The Four Secret Rings of Love and Happiness* helped propel this project in fast gear.

I also have to give recognition to my aunt Geatane Hains, head of the Hains family, for her support by reviewing and providing countless suggestions for improving the voice behind the message.

Our Creator gave me a second opportunity to share His love and blessing with the world. He is the one who ultimately inspired me to continue writing about his message of love and happiness.

Then, always to my grandparents, Henry and Rose Hains. I owe them my current blessings.

Your time is limited, so don't waste it living someone else's life. Don't be trapped by dogma – which is living with the results of other people's thinking. Don't let the noise of others' opinions drown out your own inner voice. And most important, have the courage to follow your heart and intuition.

- Steve Jobs

Introduction

Take a good look at the bride on the cover of this book. What do you see? Happiness? Contentment? Love? Perhaps you see only an impossible dream. Well, dreams come true and this book is a testament to it. The beautiful bride on the cover is my wife on the day of our wedding. She worked on herself, on her self-love, for five years before she was ready to meet someone, me, online! The good news is that you don't have to spend five years working on personal grow before you meet your soulmate. It takes only 21 days of dedication to self-love to be ready to meet your soulmate.

I assume that you've been meeting dates. More specifically, you've been meeting dates online—or trying to. You've been doing this for eons and eons... and you're running out of excuses as to why you haven't found a partner yet.

It's getting so your knee-jerk response to "Why are you still single?" is not something that can be said in polite company.

YOU'VE HAD IT UP TO HERE...

Not only that, but you're losing interest. You don't want to read come-ons from people who can't use a capital letter, or people who clearly haven't read your profile. You've come to expect the 20-year difference between the profile picture and the person waiting for you in the coffee shop, and you are utterly blasé about claims of financial-prowess and stock images of full bookcases.

WHY IS IT SO *FREAKING* COMPLICATED?

You're almost at the end of your rope... but you are not the sort of person who can live as a chaste hermit, and you don't know what else to do. You feel that time is literally running out (unless some wizard finally breaks the code on immortality potions).

The Flower doesn't dream of the bee.
It blossoms and the bee comes.

-Mark Nepo

You're dreaming of the perfect relationship where you are loved for who you truly are (self-love) and that you have amazing *selfless* sex every day (intimacy). You want to find that ideal partner who can express their feelings without disrespecting you or being disengaged (communication). You want to find someone who shares your values and has a similar vision of your future together (common values and goals).

If you think that the previous four fundamentals are impossible to find in one person at the same time... then you are wrong! You *can* find that person! You just need to be the vessel that welcomes these attributes.

This cleansing program will do this for you!

IT IS TIME TO RECALIBRATE YOUR LOVE COMPASS!

This time-tested cleansing program will re-center your spirit so you can meet the person of your dreams—and, yes, that person exists. Countless people have found their fairytale story online. You can do it too!

Online dating *can* be the relationship breakthrough that you need: it's easy to meet people, efficient, and clean. It doesn't involve sitting through set-up dinners or blind dates arranged by well-intentioned friends. A double swipe clarifies attraction.

Here is the solution.

I want to send you on the date of your life. You deserve it, after all. You will fly to Paris and spend the next four weeks being in love—with yourself, that is.

Why Paris?

Why not?

This city is known for its romantic scenery and *joie de vivre*. Imagine yourself dining, dancing, walking beneath the stars with the perfect soulmate: YOU!

As you experience everything there is about this magical city, you're going to lock in your love for yourself, just like lovers do with love-locks on the Pont des Arts, Paris. Why love-locks? They demonstrate your commitment to yourself. They prove your focus on your self-love. Your love-locks are good for *you*. 🔒

First, we will establish and review your past relationship patterns. This step is critical in order to find out where you need to make peace before you are able to move forward into your new relationship. We will spend some time near *la Seine,* sipping a *café au lait.* You will tell me about all your past relationships, and we will find out the common thread, the pattern. You may already know it!

Then we will expand on that breakthrough and focus on what you want in your next relationship. We will focus on your big WHY and establish S.M.A.R.T. goals. You are going to harness the power of focus and written commitment.

We will have picnic near the *Bois de Boulogne* and we will discover how you relate to your secrets—that is, your Four Secrets of Love and Happiness. This section will identify areas that require your attention.

Finally, as you walk down *Champs Élysées*, taking time to shop at Louis Vuitton or admiring the *Musée d'Orsay*, you will journal your transformation.

Over the next 21 days, you will go from the chrysalis stage to a magnificent butterfly—so light, so happy. No dating sites, no physical dating, no texting to attention seekers, and no booty call. In fact, every time you go back to your old self, you will need to re-start this cleansing from day one.

You will love yourself like you never have before.

I strongly recommend you exercise self-appreciation every day to reconnect your body to your soul. Establish a daily period of self-appreciation where you will love your body and give it amazing pleasure, just like you would give to your soulmate. I invite you to review my French Amour™ products.

These have been tested and approved for the greatest quality and performance.

This cleansing is mostly for your soul; however, I suggest you also cleanse your body, as the outside should match the inside. (You know the saying about dressing for the job you want? The same applies to relationships!) French Amour™ has an amazing line of products to help with this.

I've written this program for you so you can use, and not being abused by, online dating sites to find your soulmate.

For the past 20 years, I've help countless singles and couples live and experience a healthy relationship. Being a Couple and Relationship Psychotherapist, I only focus on what matter in a healthy relationship. Based on decades and decades of study and clinical researches, I focus on the four fundamentals, "The Secrets", of any healthy relationship. It is nearly impossible to experience a healthy relationship without self-love, intimacy, communication, and common goals and values. I strongly encourage you to read *The Four Secret Rings of Love and Happiness*. It is the perfect complement to this program.

Take this journey with me, and you'll learn what you need to know to find the person of your dream.

You will learn the following:

-Discover the relationship patterns that hold you back from happiness.

-Know and visualize exactly who will be the prince or princess of your dream with the S.M.A.R.T. tool.

-Discover which of the Four Secrets are your strengths and which are the ones you need to work on.

-Know exactly which person you want to attract, and the areas of your personality that require your attention for the next 21 days.

-Get rid of that personality trait that holds you back from living the perfect love story.

-and so much more.

Did you know…

In February 2017, Match.com™ published a study that showed 15% of singles are addicted to the process of looking for a date, and they are 125% more likely to admit to feeling addicted to dating than older generations admit.

(http://www.multivu.com/players/English/8024551-match-7th-annual-singles-in-america-study/)

The dopamine released in the brain is the problem: people become addicted to that high, and they don't want to take it to the next level (which involves norepinephrine, which causes the thrill people feel when falling in love).

Another study (http://www.huffingtonpost.com/greg-hodge/online-dating-lies_b_1930053.html) suggests that 53% of people lie on their dating profiles. Right away, this puts the relationship at risk, as the match is not accurate, communication is blocked, and the partners already resent the other for lying and wasting their time.

Do not feel that you have to lie about who you are, ever again. Knowing yourself will help you know exactly who will be your perfect partner for life—your best friend forever.

There will be no need to stop at the first relationship high. There are more and better highs coming—I promise!

Ten minutes per day will change your life. Do you have 10 minutes a day to live the happiness life ever?

Make online dating a breeze and find that partner who's perfect for *you*.

Break the addiction to the initial attraction and prepare yourself for the other magnificent experiences of a relationship with your soulmate.

One month can be a magical period. Scientific studies have proven that even the worst habits can be broken in that time, and that the new habits are established for life.

When humans don't have close relationships with others, there's no intimacy. Lack of intimacy causes loneliness. Loneliness causes physical and mental damage, long-term health problems, and premature aging.

DO YOU REALLY WANT TO LIVE A LONELY LIFE?

THEN TAKE ACTION. TAKE ACTION NOW.

NEVER ALLOW YOURSELF TO BE A VICTIM OF YOUR PAST. I GIVE YOU THE TOOLS TO BE HAPPY AND BE IN LOVE.

ALL YOU HAVE TO DO IS TO TAKE CHARGE OF YOUR LIFE, NOW!

SHOW ALL THE "DEAD BEATS" WHO YOU TRULY ARE AND WHAT YOU CAN DO!

I CHALLENGE YOU!

Before you begin this journey, hit "pause" on all your online dating accounts. Yes, all of them. Ignore the message boxes that are full of suggestive photographs and thoughtless pick-up lines. Don't rate "just one more profile".

It's not "stop". It's just "pause".

Have you done that? Good.

Now, come with me. You're going to take yourself on a date.

It's going to be the best date you've ever been on.

It's in Paris !

Discovering Your Relationship Patterns
-
The key to releasing the control over your love life.

One of the most important aspects of any relationship (and your love life, in general) is to discover and understand your relationship patterns. You may ask why it's important that this be addressed during this cleansing program. As with everything in life, knowledge is power. Understanding and releasing your pattern will help you focus on the perfect relationship, so you don't end up going back to the same road of unhappy relationships.

Let's define a relationship pattern. A pattern is simply an internal representation of what a relationship should look and feel like for you. This "blueprint" is most often created during childhood and reinforced with accumulated relationship experiences. It is typically what you saw, or how you interpreted, your parents' interaction with each other in all the spheres of their relationship. This *internalization* will play a major role in how you communicate, experience your sex life, work with your partner, etc. These patterns also play a significant role in finding a partner who is "comfortable", who is in-line with your pattern and vice-versa.

These patterns are known as *the love compass*. That love compass keeps you within your comfort zone and the familiarity known to date.

However, the problem occurs when you internalize some dysfunctional relationship habits that prevent you from finding that perfect partner. Let's say, for example, that, growing up, you saw your parents giving each other "the silent treatment" or screaming at each other instead of effectively communicating their problems or frustrations. In turn, you became accustomed of this pattern for resolving conflicts. Unless you are fine being with an emotionally abusive partner, the chance is great that you will attract this type of personality. I could give you countless examples related to this subject, but I think you get the point. The most important thing is to be aware of your relationship pattern and decide if that is what you want in your next relationship.

Until you heal your past, your life patterns and relationships will continue to be the same. It's just the faces that change.

- Anonymous

Let's start having some "ah-ha!" moments, shall we?

Make yourself a lovely cup of *café au lait* or pour yourself a glass of French wine, and find a comfortable table for writing. Pretend you are sitting with me beside *la Seine*. The water burbles by, and fashionable people stroll in front of our café. There are distant sounds of the city, but you and I are sitting together, and you can hear my voice clearly as I ask you about your past relationships. I am non-judgmental. I do not blame your past choices. We are just trying to find clarity in the truth. Trust my voice, and trust the honesty of your responses.

Ready? Take a sip, and we'll begin.

On our journey to find your pattern, you will focus on the past 3 to 5 romantic relationships you've had. This should give you some perspective on your recurring love life patterns.

Please write down the following information:

Describe the "look" or physical type of your past relationships. Were they tall or petit, slight or muscular, blond or dark? Make sure you include their name.

1)
....
....
....

2)
....
....
....

3)
....
....
....

4)
....
....
....

5)
....
....
....

Describe the personality characteristics that first attracted you. Were they witty or serious, intense or charming, passionate or go-the-flow? Were they highly intellectual or did they prefer the simple life?

1)
....
....
....

2)
....
....
....

3)
....
....
....

4)
....
....
....

5)
....
....
....

Please tell me what first attracted you to each person. What was *the* thing that really made you "hot" for this individual.

1)
....
....
....

2)
....
....
....

3)
....
....
....

4)
....
....
....

5)
....
....
....

Take a minute here and reflect on your answers. Do you start to see a pattern, a common denominator around the type of person you are attracting or attracted to?

When you think back on these past relationships, how would you describe the level of maturity? How were they at being accountable or assuming responsibility for their actions, good or bad? Parallel to this answer, how would you qualify your own level of maturity when assuming responsibility within each relationship?

1)
....
....
....

2)
....
....
....

3)
....
....
....

4)
....
....
....

5)
....
....
....

"I'm only responsible for what I say, not for what you understand" is the biggest cop-out in history.

Reflecting on your past sex life or intimacy, how would you describe your level of compatibility in each of these past relationships?

1)
....
....
....

2)
....
....
....

3)
....
....
....

4)
....
....
....

5)
....
....
....

How would you describe your communication style within the past relationships? What is the number one thing that comes to mind when you think about communicating difficult and emotional messages to your partner?

1)
....
....
....

2)
....
....
....

3)
....
....
....

4)
....
....
....

5)
....
....
....

Sex is often referred as the "glue" that keeps the connection of souls between partners. Sex is the most exhilarating human experience, but only if both partners have the same values or vision of its outcome.

Did you spend time talking about your personal values and goals in your relationship? Did you feel that you shared core values? Did you have common goals with clear timelines?

1)
....
....
....

2)
....
....
....

3)
....
....
....

4)
....
....
....

5)
....
....
....

Did you know:
Assuming responsibility, good or bad, is the number #1 cause of happiness. When you assume responsibility for your current life, you stop being a victim of it!

When you think back on these relations, what was the number 1 "red flag" that caused the break-up? What caused the break-up and who initiated the "rupture"?

1)
....
....
....

2)
....
....
....

3)
....
....
....

4)
....
....
....

5)
....
....
....

Reflecting on all your answers, What are your 5 "Ah-ha!" moments?

1)
....
....
....

2)
....
....
....

3)
....
....
....

4)
....
....
....

5)
....
....
....

Broken patterns = broken chains.

Describe 5 relationship patterns that you now see. Are they in-line with your perfect relationship? If not, why?

1)
....
....
....

2)
....
....
....

3)
....
....
....

4)
....
....
....

5)
....
....
....

"Embrace your womanality." BE YOU! Men love the power of a woman's true body.

- Andrea L.K. Hains

The Four Secret Rings of Love and Happiness

-

Discover your secrets!

French Amour™ gives insight into the *je ne sais quoi* that makes romance seem elusive.

I strongly recommend reading *The Four Secret Rings of Love and Happiness*. It clarifies the simple approach to an amazing relationships.

Here's a summary:

- 🔒 First Ring: Self-Love
- 🔒 Second Ring: Intimacy
- 🔒 Third Ring: Communication
- 🔒 Fourth Ring: Goals and Values

This journal will help you focus on the First Ring.

Self-Love.

Why are we focusing on this Secret Ring?

The first secret, self-love, is the main problem with online dating sites. Society and the sites themselves encourage us to display a limited profile of ourselves. The demand to appear perfect, to hide anything we're not proud of, limits our ability to communicate clearly.

You are perfect. Are you model-thin, 21 years old, shiny-haired, and astoundingly intelligent? Maybe not, but that does not mean you are not the perfect *you*.

The Perfect You

Communication, the third Secret Ring, is key to a good relationship.

If you're going to go on a date with yourself, you need to communicate well. Honesty is the life-blood you're looking for.

There are four sins of communication:

- Being critical
- Being disrespectful
- Being defensive
- Being disengaged

Are you guilty of any of these when communicating with yourself? Think about your online dating profile.

If you've tweaked (or downright lied about) your age, your weight, or your interests, you've done so because you're critical and/or defensive.

If you've left out an interest or hobby because you're embarrassed about it, you've disengaged from your true self.

If you've minimized or ignored a strong value or belief of yours, you've been disrespectful to yourself.

Before you go on your Parisian date we will do an exercise about honesty and self-love.

Please undress completely and look at your full image in a tall mirror. What do *you* love about what you see? Turn slowly, still looking at yourself. Which attributes of your body do you really like? Do you love your body? Are you comfortable being naked and looking at yourself in the mirror?

If you are unable to see the beauty of your own body, return to the mirror. The French artists have painted many bodies that would not fly on a Hollywood screen, yet—even hundreds of years later—we still view these artists' models as beautiful.

Keep looking in the mirror until you can see what Renoir and Matisse would have seen in you.

Now, do you feel ready to spend the next 21 days on date in Paris with yourself and be ready to find your soulmate when you come back? If not, let's go, anyway. This is the perfect occasion to take action.

No excuse, no justification, and no criticisms. Just raise your hand and commit *with action* to do something about it.

If you are happy, that's perfect. Love your body every day, so you can tell your soulmate how much you love it.

Become a magnet for love and positivity, and everyone to be attracted to you.

Beauty - be not caused - It is

- Emily Dickinson

Over the next two days, complete this profile - honestly.

Full name: ....

Birthdate: ....

Age: ....

Height: ....

Weight: ....

Body shape: ....

True hair colour: ....

True eye colour: ....

True skin tone: ....

This is who you really are. You might color your hair or wear make-up, but the true you is the perfect you. This is the self you need to love.

Love-Lock It 🔒

This is who I am.

Copy this statement. Write it, so you remember it in mind, body, and soul. ✍

....

....

Hiding the true you from yourself means you will hide it from others.

They will be interacting with a facade, unable to see reality clearly.

There is nothing wrong with who you are. Love who you are.

Now, it's time to work on who you want to be and the relationship you want to attract.

Remember, there's nothing wrong with who and what you are now. That said, something's not working the way you want it to, or else you wouldn't have this journal in your hands.

There is a gap between what you want in a relationship and what you are attracting or experiencing. This is what you need to address!

Based on the previous chapter on patterns and being truly honest with yourself, What do you think you need to improve? Write it down:

Thank you for sharing.

Tell me more... How are you feeling right now? Relieved? Angry? Ashamed? Joyous? Happy? ✍

The big WHY and S.M.A.R.T goals

What you think is a problem might not be the problem. Sometimes, people look outside themselves for solutions, when everything you need is right there inside you.

Love-Lock It 🔒

I have all the tools I need to be the master of my own destiny.

Copy this statement. Write it, so you remember it in mind, body, and soul. ✎

....
....

I'm going to help you do a little self-exploration. This will help you organize your thoughts, select relevant goals, and plan your journey to get the relationship of your dream.

Let's get started!

We have taken an elegant little picnic to the *Bois de Boulogne*, a lovely park in Paris. It's part of an ancient oak forest and was once the hunting grounds of French kings. Some of the trees are over a hundred years old, and people row quiet boats beneath their shade. We sit on a thick, soft blanket, eating cold finger food and drinking chilled wine.

As you think about the difficult topics that come next, imagine yourself lying on the blanket, looking at the blue sky through the leaves of the trees. Breathe the fresh air, and acknowledge your pain *and* your strength, as well as the beauty of life.

You are not alone with your unhappiness. If the gorgeous setting suddenly seems to disappear and you are only left with your agony, listen to my voice, and remember that I am sitting right beside you. Together, we can get through this journey and see the beautiful light at the other end.

Your Love Compass

Every journey leading to personal growth and finding the love of your life starts with the question **WHY**. The bigger and brighter the **WHY**, the greater the chance you will be successful in achieving your goals. The **WHY** represents the motivation behind your need to grow and find love. Your personal growth and evolution through this process is your ultimate goal.

Love-Lock It 🔒

By understanding why I want something, I can set a clear path to the goal.

Copy this statement. Write it, so you remember it in mind, body, and soul. ✎

....
....

Your **WHY** could be that you've experienced a terrible break-up and never want to feel that kind of pain again. It could be that you can't seem to find the person you are meant to be with, or it may simply be the dream of a happy relationship that you always wanted to see come true.

Please take the time, right now, to write down **WHY** are you are embarking on this journey. Make sure to describe in great detail the *pain* that you are currently experiencing.

Write down all of your emotions. Be thorough, be specific and, most importantly, be honest.

<u>I cannot emphasize strongly enough the importance of this initial phase</u>.

Write down your pain. Give this journal your pain so it can be used for positive changes in your life:

Tell me about the pain that pushes you and motivates you to want to change something in your life. Describe your big WHY. ✎

> *Just as women's bodies are softer than men's, so their understanding is sharper.*
>
> *- Christine de Pizan*

Thank you for sharing.

Tell me more... How are you feeling right now? Relieved? Angry? Ashamed? Joyous? Happy? ✍

Now that you know your **WHY** and the pain associated with this decision, it is time to take these two elements and **create a path towards your happiness**.

Love-Lock It 🔒

Chaos within the heart is not compatible with order in the mind.

Copy this statement. Write it, so you remember it in mind, body, and soul. ✎

....
....

You may have heard the acronym S.M.A.R.T. before. S.M.A.R.T. goal-setting allows you to track your progress toward your objective by ensuring every goal is **S**pecific, **M**easurable, **A**ttainable, **R**elevant, and **T**ime-bound. Without this structure, goals are merely a desire with no propulsion or direction. Be prepared to provide what you will give in return for achieving this goal. What are the actions you are ready to commit to in order to achieve this goal?

Let's take few minutes to define your goal. What do you really want out of this journey toward love and happiness? Identify your goal in one sentence. Make sure to include the counterpart: **your actions**.

Example:

I want to find the person of my dreams within six months of today (dd/mm/y). This person will be everything I wanted. Not only will this person be beautiful, generous, funny, and kind but we will fall in love immediately and plan our life together.

Now it's your turn! Describe your path to happiness—and be specific. This is your first step. This is a big portion of your **WHY**, the problem you are trying to resolve.

Tell me... and be specific.

Now take that goal and set a measure (a specific solution) that will send you on your way to achieve this goal.

Tell me... and set a measure so you know you are on the right track to accomplishing your goal. ✑

Example:

In the six months following my acceptance of self-love, I will meet a minimum of six new potential partners who share my goals and values, and with whom I believe I can have a good relationship. I will journal each experience with these people so I have a clear memory of how we interacted. I will then feel comfortable deleting my profiles on all the current dating sites.

Love-Lock It 🔒

Actions speak louder than word. I plan and take massive actions to accomplish my goal!

Copy this statement. Write it, so you remember it in mind, body, and soul. ✍

....
....

Now that you have a specific goal and have added some measure, it's time to make sure it is attainable. Being attainable means that the goal is realistic for you. You need to be careful, so you're not setting yourself up for failure right from the start.

Example:

I will head to bed 20 minutes earlier every night, so I have ample time to write in this journal. This is not a problem because I used to spend this time on online dating sites.

Tell me more... and make your goal realistic for you. ✎

It's time to think about the relevance of this goal from the perspective of solving your problem. You need to ask yourself, "Does this goal really help solve my **WHY** and alleviate the pain that I have?" Ask yourself how this solution will help you advance towards solving your **WHY** and bring you closer to achieving your goal.

Example:

I have been flirting with anyone who has an attractive profile photo and a car. The person I am online doesn't match the person I am in real life.

Tell me about the relevance of this goal to solve my **WHY**, my pain.

Love-Lock It 🔒

Being self-aware of my mistakes means I can stop making the mistakes.

Copy this statement. Write it, so you remember it in mind, body, and soul.

We are at the final stage of our S.M.A.R.T. goal-setting. The actions that you have determined will propel you towards solving your WHY must be set into motion in a timely fashion.

Example:

By focusing on myself for a month, I will know precisely what sort of a person I want to spend my time with.

or

I will work on my self-love every day for the next 21 days. After that period, I will invest 30 minutes a day in finding my ideal partner online.

Tell me... and detail a timeframe in which you will achieve your goal. ✍

As with any good communication, you need to summarize. Please write down your details.

Specific: Is it clear and well-articulated?

Measurable: What will tell me if I am progressing in the right direction?

Attainable: Am I setting myself for success?

Relevant: Will it address my **Why** in a big way?

Time-bound: What is my time-frame to accomplish this big goal?

Tell me.

Voilà!

You are now well underway on your journey. Your path to happiness is set! Take some time to let that feeling sink in. Knowing exactly what you want to do is the single **MOST** important step on your journey. Now that you have clearly described who you will be and what you want to achieve in the near future, there is no place to hide and no excuses.

Love-Lock It 🔒

Of course I can do it!

Copy this statement. Write it, so you remember it in mind, body, and soul.

....

....

Your journey to The Four Secret Rings of Love and Happiness involves taking one step at the time and trusting yourself that you made the right decision. You must believe, ***without doubt***, that action always cures a problem.

Now that you have identified your destination, the following section will determine your path, the route that will lead you to your happy ending. This next section will review the Four Secrets in detail, so you can evaluate which areas are your strongest and which ones need your attention.

It is better to be led by your dreams than pushed by your problems.

The First Secret Ring: Self-Love
-
The foundation of all destinations

It can be easy to fall into the "I'm unlovable" trap.

You are not unlovable. On the contrary, you are entirely lovable. I promise you this.

I want you to trust me. Focus on loving and cherishing yourself, and you'll discover that your heart is not ice, nor is it murky darkness. You are a beautiful soul with a lovely warm heart. You have *so much* to give! But to share it to someone, you must first realize what it is.

In your life, everything starts and ends within you. You are the soil that nourishes all the aspects of your life. Self-love is that fertile ground. It is all about the love in you, for you! Self-love is the foundation of any and every healthy relationship. Let's assess the areas that need your attention.

Love-Lock It 🔒

I love myself.

Copy this statement. Write it, so you remember it in mind, body, and soul.

....

....

Assessment

The following steps are very important. Please follow them carefully.

Step One - Read the statement.

Step Two - Rate the statement from 1 to 10 (1 being not at all true for you, and 10 being absolutely true for you). Please indicate the date on which you made this rating. It may change over time, especially with low scores.

Step Three - After reading each statement and rating it, provide a few sentences that support your rating. Once more, your perception may change over time.

It is also a good idea to review and revaluate these answers every month or so. If you are diligent about your journey to The Four Secret Rings of Love and Happiness, you will see a transformation happening right before your eyes—a transformation led by love.

Remember that we are still on the fresh green grass of the *Bois de Boulogne*. What you have learned about yourself has made the lines sharper, the colors stronger. Your understanding is giving you more control than you've ever had.

Self-Love

#1 Self-Responsibility: You are at the center of everything that happens to you. This first principle of self-love is paramount to all self-development. Without it, your journey will stagnate. Think about these statements:

I am response-ABLE. I take full responsibility of my current situation and my ability to be who I really want to be.

1st Rating: ____/10   Date: (mm / dd / yy)

Tell me more. ✍

I am response-ABLE. I take full responsibility of my current situation and my ability to be who I really want to be.

2nd Rating: 10   Date: (mm / dd / yy)

Tell me more. ✍

Love-Lock It 🔒

I am in control of everything I do and say, as well as everything I do not do or do not say.

Copy this statement. Write it, so you remember it in mind, body, and soul. ✎

....
....

I am always able to determine my part in every success or failure, in any situation.

1st Rating: _____/10 *Date: (mm / dd / yy)*

Tell me more. ✎

I am always able to determine my part in every success or failure, in any situation.

2nd Rating: ____/10   *Date:* (mm / dd / yy)

Tell me more.

I do not blame, criticize, complain, or feel like a victim.

1ˢᵗ Rating: ____/10   Date: (mm / dd / yy)

Tell me more. ✎

I do not blame, criticize, complain, or feel like a victim.

2nd Rating: ..../10   Date: (mm / dd / yy)

Tell me more. ✑

Self-Love

#2 Self-Affirmation: We get wrapped up in negative thoughts and forget about all the good things we have. Make time to see the beauty, love, kindness, and happiness that's in your life. Think about these statements:

Every day I remind myself about, or write in my journal, five blessings or things I am grateful for.

1st Rating: ____/10   Date: (mm / dd / yy)

Tell me more. ✍

Every day I remind myself, or write in my journal, about five blessings or things I am grateful for.

2nd Rating: ____/10   Date: (mm / dd / yy)

Tell me more. ✍

Every day, I find new ways to be grateful.

1st Rating: ____/10   Date: (mm / dd / yy)

Tell me more. ✍

Love-Lock It 🔒

What I have are the things I once hoped for; what I hope for now, I will have in the future.

Copy this statement. Write it, so you remember it in mind, body, and soul. ✐

....
....

Every day, I find new ways to be grateful.

2nd Rating: _____/10   Date: (mm / dd / yy)

Tell me more. ✐

I have an object or reminder (like the French Amour™ silver ring) that I use to trigger my self-affirmation every morning.

1st Rating: ____/10 Date: (mm / dd / yy)

Tell me more. ✐

I have an object or reminder (like the French Amour™ silver ring) that I use to trigger my self-affirmation every morning.

2nd Rating: _____/10   *Date:* (mm / dd / yy)

Tell me more. ✍

I know which main areas I am focusing on for my daily self-affirmation (e.g., money, health, career, family, friends).

1st *Rating:* ____/10   *Date: (mm / dd / yy)*

Tell me more. ✍

I know which main areas I am focusing on for my daily self-affirmation (e.g., money, health, career, family, friends).

2nd Rating: ____/10 *Date: (mm / dd / yy)*

Tell me more. ✑

Self-Love

#3 Self-Improvement: If you only eat what you need for survival, you will only survive; to thrive, you must occasionally eat a little extra food. Make sure you remember to fertilize body, mind, and soul. Make sure that goal is reasonable and attainable.

Every day, I remind myself of my personal improvement goal for the day.

1st Rating: ____/10   Date: (mm / dd / yy)

Tell me more. ✐

Every day, I remind myself of my personal improvement goal for the day.

2nd Rating: ____*/10 Date: (mm / dd / yy)*

Tell me more. ✍

Daily, I take some time to reflect on the areas of my personality that need to be improved and set S.M.A.R.T. (Specific, Measurable, Achievable, Relevant, and Timely) goals for their achievement.

1st Rating: ____/10   Date: (mm / dd / yy)

Tell me more. ✍

Daily, I take some time to reflect on the areas of my personality that need to be improved and set SMART (Specific, Measurable, Achievable, Relevant, and Timely) goals for their achievement.

2nd Rating: ____/10   Date: (mm / dd / yy)

Tell me more. ✍

Love-Lock It 🔒

Determination is the fuel of achievement.

Copy this statement. Write it, so you remember it in mind, body, and soul. ✍

....
....

I pursue my personal goals or objectives until I succeed.

1st Rating: ____/10   Date: (mm / dd / yy)

Tell me more. ✍

....
....
....
....
....
....
....
....
....
....
....
....
....
....
....
....
....

I pursue my personal goals or objectives until I succeed.

2nd Rating: ____/10   Date: (mm / dd / yy)

Tell me more. ✍

I have a clear vision of the goals that I want to achieve in the next month, six-months, and year.

1st Rating: ____/10 *Date: (mm / dd / yy)*

Tell me more.

I have a clear vision of the goals that I want to achieve in the next month, six-months, and year.

2nd Rating: ____*/10   Date: (mm / dd / yy)*

Tell me more. ✍

Love-Lock It 🔒

If I serve it up, I can take it. Bring it on.

Copy this statement. Write it, so you remember it in mind, body, and soul. ✍

....
....

I create my life to be exactly the way I want it to be.

1st Rating: ____/10   Date: (mm / dd / yy)

Tell me more. ✍

....
....
....
....
....
....
....
....
....
....
....
....
....
....
....
....
....
....

I create my life to be exactly the way I want it to be.

2nd Rating: ..../10 *Date:* (mm / dd / yy)

Tell me more.. ✍

Self-Love

#4 Self-Forgiveness: Grudges and resentment take up a lot of space and are dead weight. Getting rid of them leaves room for love and happiness. Forgive others, and forgive yourself.

Every day, before bedtime, I take few minutes to forgive the people and events that hurt me that day. I also take some time to forgive myself for the mistakes I've made or my perceived shortcomings.

1st Rating: ____/10 Date: (mm / dd / yy)

Tell me more. ✍

Every day, before bedtime, I take few minutes to forgive the people and events that hurt me that day. I also take some time to forgive myself for the mistakes I've made or my perceived shortcomings.

2nd Rating: ____/10   Date: (mm / dd / yy)

Tell me more. ✍

I am able to let go. I am able to release any negative emotions inside of me.

1st Rating: ____/10 *Date:* (mm / dd / yy)

Tell me more.

I am able to let go. I am able to release any negative emotions inside of me.

2nd Rating: ____/10   *Date:* (mm / dd / yy)

Tell me more. ✍

Love-Lock It 🔒

Clinging tightly to the past makes it very difficult to move forward to the future.

Copy this statement. Write it, so you remember it in mind, body, and soul. ✍

....
....

I do not seek revenge or hold resentment, but rather forgive the person who hurt me. I understand that I am response-able for anything and everything that happens around me.

1st Rating: ____/10 *Date:* (mm / dd / yy)

Tell me more. ✍

....
....
....
....
....
....
....
....
....
....
....
....
....
....

I do not seek revenge or hold resentment, but rather forgive the person that who me. I understand that I am response-able for anything and everything that happens around me.

2nd Rating: ____*/10   Date: (mm / dd / yy)*

Tell me more. ✍

Love-Lock It 🔒

I am worthy of the compliments I give myself.

Copy this statement. Write it, so you remember it in mind, body, and soul. ✍

....

....

Self-Love

#5 Self-Appreciation: You are a gift from your Creator. There is nothing inherently wrong with you. Appreciate what you have and what you are. Appreciate your connections with the Universe.

You probably say something nice about other people several times a day. Humans do that for each other, so that the good things are clearly acknowledged.

You need to do this for yourself, too—not just for other people. You need to compliment the good things about yourself, focus on them, deliberately hone them.

Love-Lock It 🔒

By clarifying the good things about myself, I learn to never give those things up.

Copy this statement. Write it, so you remember it in mind, body, and soul. ✍

....
....

I can lift myself up

or

I can tear myself down.

Every day, I take time to appreciate my mind, body, and soul.

1st Rating: ____/10   *Date: (mm / dd / yy)*

Tell me more. ✍

Every day, I take time to appreciate my mind, body, and soul.

2nd Rating: ____/10   Date: (mm / dd / yy)

Tell me more. ✎

Every day, I make an effort to keep my mind happy, to keep my intellect stimulated.

1st Rating: ____/10 Date: (mm / dd / yy)

Tell me more. Describe your favourite self-appreciation for your mind. ✎

Every day, I make an effort to keep my mind happy, to keep my intellect stimulated.

2nd Rating: ____/10   Date: (mm / dd / yy)

Tell me more. Describe any new approaches you have to this aspect of self-appreciation. ✍

Every day, I do something to keep my soul happy.

1st Rating: _____/10   Date: (mm / dd / yy)

Tell me more. Describe your favourite self-appreciation for your soul. ✍

Every day, I do something to keep my soul happy.

2nd Rating: ____/10 Date: (mm / dd / yy)

Tell me more. List any new activities you do for your soul's happiness. ✍

Love-Lock It 🔒

My body carries me, my mind, my soul. I need to acknowledge that.

Copy this statement. Write it, so you remember it in mind, body, and soul. ✎

....
....

Every day, I appreciate my body.

1ˢᵗ Rating: ____/10 *Date:* (mm / dd / yy)

Tell me more. Describe your favourite self-appreciation for your body. ✎

....
....
....
....
....
....
....
....
....
....
....
....
....
....
....
....
....

Every day, I appreciate my body.

2nd Rating: _____/10 *Date: (mm / dd / yy)*

Tell me more. Describe your favourite self-appreciation for your body. ✍

This completes your introspection on self-love. This is by far the MOST important aspect of ANY relationship, because *you* are the heart of everything you do. You inject soul and energy into every relationship you have, no matter how insignificant the relationship may seem.

Now, you *own* self-love. You can give love because you possess it. You know what love looks like for yourself, and you'll be able to see it in other people.

Love-Lock It 🔒

Understanding is far deeper than knowledge.

Copy this statement. Write it, so you remember it in mind, body, and soul.

....
....

What did you learn about your self-love? Please summarize your "Ah-ha!" moments.

Tell me.

....
....
....
....
....
....
....
....

The Second Secret Ring: Intimacy

-

Communion of souls

The word *intimacy* comes from the Latin word that means "to make known". When you make yourself known to someone, and they make themselves known to you, you become *intimate*.

You must be intimate with yourself before you can be intimate with someone else.

Intimacy comes in three forms. It consists of emotional, spiritual, and physical intimacy.

The first principle of intimacy is critical. You need to accept your emotions, your beliefs and values, and your desires.

Communication is an integral part of intimacy. Communicate well with yourself. Be honest, be open, be non-judgemental. Be kind to yourself.

Intimacy

#1 Emotional Intimacy: Emotional intimacy means the ability to be intimate with your own emotions as well as another person's. It is the ability to recognize them and feel safe with them. You should be able to express them through your daily journal without fear.

Love-Lock It 🔒

Vulnerability creates strength.

Copy this statement. Write it, so you remember it in mind, body, and soul. ✍

....
....

The opposite of loneliness is not togetherness. It's intimacy.
— *Richard Bach*

Rate the following statements, as you did for the First Ring of Love and Happiness (self-love).

I can say my most inner thoughts to myself.

1st Rating: ____/10   *Date:* (mm / dd / yy)

Tell me more. ✍

I can say my most inner thoughts to myself.

2nd *Rating: ____/10   Date: (mm / dd / yy)*

Tell me more.

I feel safe when I am with myself (physically, emotionally, and spiritually).

1st Rating: ____/10   *Date:* (mm / dd / yy)

Tell me more.

I feel safe when I am with myself (physically, emotionally, and spiritually).

2nd Rating: ____/10 *Date: (mm / dd / yy)*

Tell me more. ✍

I feel that I can open myself to my inner emotions and write them down in my journal, without fear.

1st Rating: ____/10   Date: (mm / dd / yy)

Tell me more.

I feel that I can open myself to my inner emotions and write them down in my journal, without fear.

2nd Rating: ____/10   *Date: (mm / dd / yy)*

Tell me more. ✍

Intimacy

#2 Spiritual Intimacy: Spiritual intimacy or romance means the ability to connect beyond the relationship. You need to connect with yourself before you can connect with someone else.

I do activities that fulfill my spiritual needs.

1st Rating: ____/10 *Date:* (mm / dd / yy)

Tell me more. ✍

I do activities that fulfill my spiritual needs.

2nd Rating: ____/10 *Date: (mm / dd / yy)*

Tell me more. List any new spiritual activities you do. ✎

Love-Lock It 🔒

Habit and tradition are taken from other people; romance is created for myself.

Copy this statement. Write it, so you remember it in mind, body, and soul. ✍

....
....

I take time to be romantic with myself.

1st Rating: ____/10   *Date:* (*mm / dd / yy*)

Tell me more. List the romantic things you do for yourself. ✍

I take time to be romantic with myself.

2nd Rating: ____/10   Date: (mm / dd / yy)

Tell me more. Are there any new ways in which you romance yourself? ✑

Intimacy

#3 Physical Intimacy: Physical intimacy, or the French Art of Love-Making, means the ability to bring courting (safety) and romance (spiritual) to the bedroom and celebrate your love yourself

I know how to physically pleasure myself.

1st Rating: ____/10   Date: (mm / dd / yy)

Tell me more. ✍

I know how to physically pleasure myself.

2nd Rating: ____/10   Date: (mm / dd / yy)
Tell me more. What has stayed the same over the past few months, and what has changed? ✍

I know which sexual activities I enjoy with a partner.

1st Rating: ____/10   Date: (mm / dd / yy)

Tell me more. ✎

I know which sexual activities I enjoy with a partner.

2nd Rating: ____/10   Date: (mm / dd / yy)

Tell me more. Detail any new sexual activities you might enjoy with a partner. ✍

Love-Lock It 🔒

Knowledge is power. If I try it, I will know whether or not I like it.

Copy this statement. Write it, so you remember it in mind, body, and soul. ✍

When I am physically intimate with a partner, I concentrate on them. I am selfless.

1ˢᵗ Rating: _____/10 *Date:* (mm / dd / yy)

Tell me more. ✍

When I am physically intimate with a partner, I concentrate on them. I am selfless.

2nd Rating: ____/10   Date: (mm / dd / yy)

Tell me more. ✍

This completes the section on intimacy.

Summarize your thoughts on it. Before you began this journal, what were you doing well to create and maintain emotional, spiritual, and physical intimacy? Which areas needed more attention from you? What would you like to change for yourself?

Enlightenment is intimacy with all things.

— *Eihei Dogan*

The Third Secret Ring: Communication

-

The golden key

The gift of communication is sacred. Far too many relationships are destroyed by a simple miscommunication or misunderstanding.

Of course, learning to communicate with yourself is the first step in learning to communicate with others. You have to know what to say, how to say it, how to react, and how to properly end the communication.

If you are meeting people online, you can't depend on facial expressions, body language, or tone of voice. Everything is done through text, and messages are often kept short because (let's face it) apps don't lend themselves to letter-writing.

The first date is also requires a different kind of communication than you would normally have. This date involves getting to know each other and deciding whether you want to have more contact. (It's not like you'll run into each other at work every day.) This communication has to be crystal clear, honest, and equal.

Using the P.A.C.T. of communication is an effective method. It's also good practice for when you and your prospective partner will reach an emotionally charged moment, as it will help you achieve a healthy relationship.

In order to be effective, both partners must use the P.A.C.T. to convey critical information.

Love-Lock It 🔒

The four sins of communication do not communicate love.

Copy this statement. Write it, so you remember it in mind, body, and soul. ✎

....
....

The Four Sins of Communication are:

- 🔒 Being critical
- 🔒 Being disrespectful
- 🔒 Being defensive
- 🔒 Being disengaged

There is a fifth sin that is the worst of them all, and that is to emotionally flood a partner with all the sins in a single episode, without consideration for their emotional well-being.

If a potential prospect commits any of these sins, this is not the partner for you. Whether online or on a first meeting or date, politely communicate your feelings about what they've said. If they don't respond in a way that makes you feel that they've heard you, wish them well and be on your way.

A partner should be willing to make a pact to use P.A.C.T.

Here is a summary of the P.A.C.T. of communication:

<u>Preparation</u>. This is where you stay calm and think about the feelings that you are trying to convey to the person. This is not the time to blurt out the first thing that comes to mind, as that will result in miscommunication or resentment.

Preparation also means choosing the right time to communicate. Don't respond with a quick sarcastic message while you're in the elevator on the way home from work.

<u>Act</u>, and express your message sensibly. Start your communication by expressing how you feel. You should typically start with "I", and then express your feelings while providing factual context that supports your feelings.

An example would be when someone sends a message that is not overtly inappropriate but makes it clear they have not looked at your profile. Take a few deep breaths, have a glass of water, and respond to their message:

Thank you for your message. While I'm flattered by the compliment, I have clearly stated that I am not looking for someone who is interested only in my body. I feel that you have not paid enough attention to the information I communicated on my profile.

Love-Lock It 🔒

*No one is **more** important than I am. I can take time to craft my response.*

Copy this statement. Write it, so you remember it in mind, body, and soul. ✍

....

....

Sharing your feelings effectively is quite simple: stick to your emotions. Refrain from using any form of personal attack, belittling, making fun, etc. Focus on the behavior that upset you.

When you have finished sharing your emotions, let the person have some time to reflect and provide some feedback to you. This is where the "magic" happens when both partners use P.A.C.T. to communicate. A good partner will know intuitively that they need to summarize your message. Since you are not using the sins of communication or its subordinates, the person will have a much easier time being open and trying to be empathic to your feelings.

Conclude or summarize your understanding of the outcome of the communication. The ability to provide a summary of your understanding will not only show that you care about the issue but also will demonstrate that you understand the potential solution to fix the issue.

Thank you for your kind response. Here is a list of things I enjoy doing. What intellectual pursuits interest you?

Thank **you**. When you have a resolution, or have just actively listened to the person's communication, simply express your gratitude by saying "thank you". This simple action will put the final touches on the *togetherness*.

Thank you for understanding my perspective. I look forward to our future communication.

Now take a few minutes to gather your thoughts on communication, and rate these statements.

Communication must be HOT. That is Honest, Open, and Two-way.
— *Dan Oswald*

I never use the four sins of communication.

1st Rating: ____/10 Date: (mm / dd / yy)

No one is perfect: think about a time when you didn't use them, and a time when you did.

I never use the four sins of communication.

2nd Rating: ____/10   Date: (mm / dd / yy)

What has changed over the last month? What benefits have you noticed? ✍

Love-Lock It 🔒

People can't communicate with me if I don't communicate with them.

Copy this statement. Write it, so you remember it in mind, body, and soul. ✍

....
....

I use P.A.C.T. to communicate important, emotionally charged messages.

1st Rating: ____/10   *Date:* (mm / dd / yy)

Tell me more. ✍

I use P.A.C.T. to communicate important, emotionally charged messages.

2nd Rating: ____/10   *Date: (mm / dd / yy)*

Tell me more. What has changed? What hasn't? ✍

I am writing openly and honestly in this journal.

1st Rating: ____/10   Date: (mm / dd / yy)

Tell me more. ✍

I am writing openly and honestly in this journal.

2nd Rating: ____/10   Date: (mm / dd / yy)

Tell me more. What has changed? What hasn't? What topics are still difficult for you think about honestly? ✍

I believe I can communicate properly with my soulmate.

1st Rating: _____/10   *Date: (mm / dd / yy)*

Tell me more. ✍

I believe I can communicate properly with my soulmate.

2nd Rating: ____/10   *Date:* (*mm / dd / yy*)

Tell me more. What has changed? What hasn't? ✍

The Fourth Secret Ring:

Goals and Values

-

Looking at the world in the same direction

Common goals and values are at the pinnacle of every single healthy relationship. Both partners must know and feel that they are working together to achieve something bigger than themselves. Values and goals are the glue that will keep you together through good and bad times. Once more, selfishness has no place in a healthy relationship.

You will have two sets of core values and goals: one set for you as an individual, and another set for your relationship. These may not be identical to your partner's, but they must be compatible if the relationship is going to work.

You and your prospective partner must have respect for each other's values and goals, especially if they are different.

Love-Lock It 🔒

My values are my personal guide to what's right and what's wrong.

Copy this statement. Write it, so you remember it in mind, body, and soul.

....

....

It's not hard to make decisions when you know what your values are.

- Roy Disney

I can easily describe my core values, as an individual and as a partner in a relationship.

1st Rating: ____/10   Date: (mm / dd / yy)

Tell me more. Describe each set of values. ✍

I can easily describe my core values, as an individual and as a partner in a relationship.

2nd Rating: ____/10   *Date: (mm / dd / yy)*

Tell me more. Have your values changed in any way? ✍

Love-Lock It 🔒

Sharing values means, we will work for the relationship, not personal gain.

Copy this statement. Write it, so you remember it in mind, body, and soul.

....
....

I have clearly communicated my core values on my profile.

1st Rating____/10   Date: (mm / dd / yy)

Tell me more.

I have clearly communicated my core values on my profile.

2nd Rating: ____/10   Date: (mm / dd / yy)

Tell me more. ✍

Love-Lock It

Without a relationship goal, I am just wandering aimlessly.

Copy this statement. Write it, so you remember it in mind, body, and soul. ✍

....
....

I can easily describe my relationship goals.

1st Rating: ____/10 *Date: (mm / dd / yy)*

Tell me more. Describe your relationship goals. ✍

I can easily describe my relationship goals.

2nd Rating: ____/10 Date: (mm / dd / yy)

Tell me more. How has your understanding of your relationship goals changed? ✑

I will work with my partner to achieve our common goals.

1st Rating: ____/10   Date: (mm / dd / yy)

Tell me more. How might you work together? ✐

I will work with my partner to achieve our common goals.

2nd Rating: ____/10   Date: (mm / dd / yy)

Tell me more. Which practices have you added or stopped? ✎

Love-Lock It 🔒

A chasm of silence is not a form of communication.

Copy this statement. Write it, so you remember it in mind, body, and soul. ✍

....
....

This concludes the section on communication. Use this page to summarize your thoughts and feelings about what you've written. (Use P.A.C.T. to make sure you're communicating clearly with yourself.) Before you began this journal, what were your communication strengths and what were your weaknesses? What will you change from now on?

....
....
....
....
....
....
....
....
....
....
....
....
....
....
....
....

Your Journal, Your Destiny

-

Your path to love and happiness

Congratulations on completing the last section! I am sure that you had to face some fears and internal resistance to bring the areas that needed your attention to light. This is an extremely important step on the road to live a happy and loving relationship. Once again, well done!

The next section is where the "magic" of journaling really takes place. You identified your relationship patterns and goal in the first part book; then you identified areas of your personality that need attention in order to achieve your goal in the second part. This final part of the book is about putting those two sections together and journaling your progress toward your goal.

As you have already taken your first steps to The Four Secret Rings of Love and Happiness, you will be asked to journal every day for the next 21 days, for a minimum of 10 minutes per day. Again, it is not the *quantity* of time that is important but the *quality* of the introspection you provide to your journal.

This journal will be a testament to your progress and transformation. No one else can do this for you. You showed courage and determination in completing the first sections.

It is now time to put everything into action.

How should you journal?

Journaling, in this particular case, is not about describing your factual life the way you might do in a diary. This is another type of journal, where memories and recollection of the day's emotions would be the focus. This one is about you and your progress in the areas that need your attention and development. It's about changing a behavior.

This is where you are focusing on self-improvement.

The first step is to identify and record the area(s) that you will be focusing on for the next 21 days. I recommend choosing only one or two critical areas. This way your progress will be easily seen, and that will be a boost to your self-confidence. (Keep your goals S.M.A.R.T.)

From the previous sections of this journal, choose two areas where you feel you need improvement. Write down the goal(s) for the next 21 days:

1. ....
....
....
....
....
....
....
....
....

2.

Why have you chosen to work on these areas? Are they simple fixes that will give you confidence or clarity, or will they have the most impact on you and your relationship(s)?

Great job. I am so proud of you! You identified your strength and areas of the Four Secrets Rings of Love and Happiness that require your attention.

> YOU HAVE FULL CONTROL OVER YOUR DESTINY AS YOU ARE THE CAPTAIN OF YOUR SHIP.
>
> MAKE MIRACLES HAPPEN IN YOUR LIFE.
>
> -Richard Henry II

Love-Lock It 🔒

I don't need to try to impress people. I am impressive in my own way.

Copy this statement. Write it, so you remember it in mind, body, and soul.

....
....

Now, take everything you've learned about the Four Rings of Love and Happiness, and apply it to your journaling for the next 21 days. Make note of the changes, the growth you see. Use the time wisely, and feel the weight lift from your shoulders. Take control. Be the perfect you.

Today you are YOU,

That is TRUER than true.

There is NO ONE alive

who is YOUER than YOU!

— *Dr. Seuss*

Before you journal each day, imagine we are strolling through Paris. Are we window shopping or in a museum? Is there soft grass beneath our feet, or smooth, cool marble? Have we stopped for another delicious drink in a café? Wherever we are, imagine you are speaking candidly to me. I will never judge you. You can be grateful for the grandest things or the tiniest, silliest things in your life. They're important to *you*, so I'm pleased that you count them as a blessing.

Take a breath before you reflect on your next self-improvement. I have taught you well, so I trust your judgment. You know what needs to be done next.

Don't think about what *I* might want you to forgive yourself for: I am not the important one here. Tell me what you have done wrong—or thought or felt—and why you need to forgive yourself for it.

As we walk along together, the movement loosens your muscles and relaxes you. There's no tension, no awkwardness. It's easy to speak to me about your day, telling me about what you did and how it made you feel. I offer my sympathy for your misfortunes, but remind you that you are response-ABLE and can deal with them. For all the good things in your day, I congratulate you and celebrate with you. I support you in your journey towards your chosen goal.

There is beauty all around us. See it as you journal your day for me.

A Date in Paris - The Online Dating Cleansing Program

Day 1.

Date: ....

Every day, I...

remind myself that I am response-able, and I assume full and entire responsibility for my day ahead. I create the outcome of my life. No one else does it for me. I am in charge, I am in control.

<u>Blessings</u> I start by putting on my French Amour™ silver ring and reminding myself of five blessings that have been bestowed upon me:

1) ....
....
2) ....
....
3) ....
....
4) ....
....
5) ....
....

<u>Self-Improvement</u> Today I will focus on...

<u>Self-Appreciation</u> Today I will appreciate my mind, body, and soul through the following activities:

Mind: ....
....
Body: ....
....
Soul: ....
....

<u>Forgiveness</u> As I remove my ring for the night, I forgive anyone who hurt me, intentionally or by accident. I forgive myself for any perceived shortcomings, as I know I've tried my best.

I forgive:

Journaling Tell me more about the feelings and emotions you've experienced throughout your day. What did you do today to take one step further toward achieving your goal and/or improving the area that needs your attention?

Love-Lock It 🔒

Lust is not love.

Copy this statement. Write it, so you remember it in mind, body, and soul. ✍

....
....

Day 2.

Date: ....

Every day, I..

remind myself that I am response-able, and I assume full and entire responsibility for my day ahead. I create the outcome of my life. No one else does it for me. I am in charge, I am in control.

<u>Blessings</u> I start by putting on my French Amour™ silver ring and reminding myself of five blessings that have been bestowed upon me:

1)...
....
2)...
....
3)...
....
4)...
....
5)...
....

<u>Self-Improvement</u> Today I will focus on...

....
....
....
....
....
....
....

<u>Self-Appreciation</u> Today I will appreciate my mind, body, and soul through the following activities:

Mind: ....
....

Body: ....
....

Soul: ....
....

<u>Forgiveness</u> As I remove my ring for the night, I forgive anyone who hurt me, intentionally or by accident. I forgive myself for any perceived shortcomings, as I know I've tried my best.

I forgive:

<u>Journaling</u> Tell me more about the feelings and emotions you've experienced throughout your day. What did you do today to take one step further toward achieving your goal and/or improving the area that needs your attention?

Love-Lock It 🔒

*A relationship should be fun **and** serious at the same time.*

Copy this statement. Write it, so you remember it in mind, body, and soul. ✍

....
....

Day 3.

Date: ....

Every day, I ....

remind myself that I am response-able, and I assume full and entire responsibility for my day ahead. I create the outcome of my life. No one else does it for me. I am in charge, I am in control.

<u>Blessings</u> I start by putting on my French Amour™ silver ring and reminding myself of five blessings that have been bestowed upon me:

1) ....
....
2) ....
....
3) ....
....
4) ....
....
5) ....
....

<u>Self-Improvement</u> Today I will focus on...

....
....
....
....
....
....
....

<u>Self-Appreciation</u> Today I will appreciate my mind, body, and soul through the following activities:

Mind: ....
....

Body: ....
....

Soul: ....
....

<u>Forgiveness</u> As I remove my ring for the night, I forgive anyone who hurt me, intentionally or by accident. I forgive myself for any perceived shortcomings, as I know I've tried my best.

I forgive:

Journaling Tell me more about the feelings and emotions you've experienced throughout your day. What did you do today to take one step further toward achieving your goal and/or improving the area that needs your attention?

Love-Lock It 🔒

A good partner will complement me, and I, them.

Copy this statement. Write it, so you remember it in mind, body, and soul. ✍

....
....

Day 4.

Date: ....

Every day, I ....

remind myself that I am response-able, and I assume full and entire responsibility for my day ahead. I create the outcome of my life. No one else does it for me. I am in charge, I am in control.

<u>Blessings</u> I start by putting on my French Amour™ silver ring and reminding myself of five blessings that have been bestowed upon me:

1) ....
....
2) ....
....
3) ....
....
4) ....
....
5) ....
....

<u>Self-Improvement</u> Today I will focus on...

....
....
....
....
....
....
....

Self-Appreciation Today I will appreciate my mind, body, and soul through the following activities:

Mind:...
....
Body:...
....
Soul:...
....

Forgiveness As I remove my ring for the night, I forgive anyone who hurt me, intentionally or by accident. I forgive myself for any perceived shortcomings, as I know I've tried my best.

I forgive:

<u>Journaling</u> Tell me more about the feelings and emotions you've experienced throughout your day. What did you do today to take one step further toward achieving your goal and/or improving the area that needs your attention?

Love-Lock It 🔒

A good relationship is not a negotiation. I don't need to "settle".

Copy this statement. Write it, so you remember it in mind, body, and soul. ✍

....
....

Day 5.

Date: ....

Every day, I..

remind myself that I am response-able, and I assume full and entire responsibility for my day ahead. I create the outcome of my life. No one else does it for me. I am in charge, I am in control.

<u>Blessings</u> I start by putting on my French Amour™ silver ring and reminding myself of five blessings that have been bestowed upon me:

1) ....
....
2) ....
....
3) ....
....
4) ....
....
5) ....
....

<u>Self-Improvement</u> Today I will focus on...

....
....
....
....
....
....
....

<u>Self-Appreciation</u> Today I will appreciate my mind, body, and soul through the following activities:

Mind: ....
....
Body: ....
....
Soul: ....
....

<u>Forgiveness</u> As I remove my ring for the night, I forgive anyone who hurt me, intentionally or by accident. I forgive myself for any perceived shortcomings, as I know I've tried my best.

I forgive:

Journaling Tell me more about the feelings and emotions you've experienced throughout your day. What did you do today to take one step further toward achieving your goal and/or improving the area that needs your attention?

Love-Lock It 🔒

Being independent does not mean that I can be my own soulmate.

Copy this statement. Write it, so you remember it in mind, body, and soul.

Day 6.

Date: ....

Every day, I ....

remind myself that I am response-able, and I assume full and entire responsibility for my day ahead. I create the outcome of my life. No one else does it for me. I am in charge, I am in control.

<u>Blessings</u> I start by putting on my French Amour™ silver ring and reminding myself of five blessings that have been bestowed upon me:

1) ....
....
2) ....
....
3) ....
....
4) ....
....
5) ....
....

<u>Self-Improvement</u> Today I will focus on...

....
....
....
....
....
....
....

<u>Self-Appreciation</u> Today I will appreciate my mind, body, and soul through the following activities:

Mind: ....
....

Body: ....
....

Soul: ....
....

<u>Forgiveness</u> As I remove my ring for the night, I forgive anyone who hurt me, intentionally or by accident. I forgive myself for any perceived shortcomings, as I know I've tried my best.

I forgive:

Journaling Tell me more about the feelings and emotions you've experienced throughout your day. What did you do today to take one step further toward achieving your goal and/or improving the area that needs your attention?

Love-Lock It 🔒

Relationships are not games. I don't need a tally board.

Copy this statement. Write it, so you remember it in mind, body, and soul. ✍

....
....

Day 7.

Date: ....

Every day, I ....

remind myself that I am response-able, and I assume full and entire responsibility for my day ahead. I create the outcome of my life. No one else does it for me. I am in charge, I am in control.

Blessings I start by putting on my French Amour™ silver ring and reminding myself of five blessings that have been bestowed upon me:

1) ....

2) ....

3) ....

4) ....

5) ....

Self-Improvement Today I will focus on...

....
....
....
....
....
....
....

<u>Self-Appreciation</u> Today I will appreciate my mind, body, and soul through the following activities:

Mind: ....
....
Body: ....
....
Soul: ....
....

<u>Forgiveness</u> As I remove my ring for the night, I forgive anyone who hurt me, intentionally or by accident. I forgive myself for any perceived shortcomings, as I know I've tried my best.

I forgive:

<u>Journaling</u> Tell me more about the feelings and emotions you've experienced throughout your day. What did you do today to take one step further toward achieving your goal and/or improving the area that needs your attention?

Love-Lock It 🔒

At some point, the dating must end, and our relationship must deepen.

Copy this statement. Write it, so you remember it in mind, body, and soul. ✍

....
....

Day 8.

Date: ....

Every day, I ....

remind myself that I am response-able, and I assume full and entire responsibility for my day ahead. I create the outcome of my life. No one else does it for me. I am in charge, I am in control.

<u>Blessings</u> I start by putting on my French Amour™ silver ring and reminding myself of five blessings that have been bestowed upon me:

1) ....
....
2) ....
....
3) ....
....
4) ....
....
5) ....
....

<u>Self-Improvement</u> Today I will focus on...

....
....
....
....
....
....
....

Self-Appreciation Today I will appreciate my mind, body, and soul through the following activities:

Mind: ....
....
Body: ....
....
Soul: ....
....

Forgiveness As I remove my ring for the night, I forgive anyone who hurt me, intentionally or by accident. I forgive myself for any perceived shortcomings, as I know I've tried my best.

I forgive:

Journaling Tell me more about the feelings and emotions you've experienced throughout your day. What did you do today to take one step further toward achieving your goal and/or improving the area that needs your attention?

Love-Lock It 🔒

A good relationship has a single, mutual voice, as well as two individual voices.

Copy this statement. Write it, so you remember it in mind, body, and soul. ✍

....
....

Day 9.

Date: ....

Every day, I ....

remind myself that I am response-able, and I assume full and entire responsibility for my day ahead. I create the outcome of my life. No one else does it for me. I am in charge, I am in control.

<u>Blessings</u> I start by putting on my French Amour™ silver ring and reminding myself of five blessings that have been bestowed upon me:

1) ....
....
2) ....
....
3) ....
....
4) ....
....
5) ....
....

<u>Self-Improvement</u> Today I will focus on...

....
....
....
....
....
....
....

<u>Self-Appreciation</u> Today I will appreciate my mind, body, and soul through the following activities:

Mind: ....

Body: ....

Soul: ....

<u>Forgiveness</u> As I remove my ring for the night, I forgive anyone who hurt me, intentionally or by accident. I forgive myself for any perceived shortcomings, as I know I've tried my best.

I forgive:

<u>Journaling</u> Tell me more about the feelings and emotions you've experienced throughout your day. What did you do today to take one step further toward achieving your goal and/or improving the area that needs your attention?

Love-Lock It 🔒

Looking and acting my best is good for my relationship with myself and with others.

Copy this statement. Write it, so you remember it in mind, body, and soul. ✍

....

....

Day 10.

Date: ....

Every day, I ....

remind myself that I am response-able, and I assume full and entire responsibility for my day ahead. I create the outcome of my life. No one else does it for me. I am in charge, I am in control.

<u>Blessings</u> I start by putting on my French Amour™ silver ring and reminding myself of five blessings that have been bestowed upon me:

1) ....
....
2) ....
....
3) ....
....
4) ....
....
5) ....
....

<u>Self-Improvement</u> Today I will focus on...

....
....
....
....
....
....
....

<u>Self-Appreciation</u> Today I will appreciate my mind, body, and soul through the following activities:

Mind: ....

Body: ....

Soul: ....

<u>Forgiveness</u> As I remove my ring for the night, I forgive anyone who hurt me, intentionally or by accident. I forgive myself for any perceived shortcomings, as I know I've tried my best.

I forgive:

<u>Journaling</u> Tell me more about the feelings and emotions you've experienced throughout your day. What did you do today to take one step further toward achieving your goal and/or improving the area that needs your attention?

Love-Lock It 🔒

Listening to advice is worthwhile, but I know myself best.

Copy this statement. Write it, so you remember it in mind, body, and soul. ✐

....
....

Day 11.

Date: ....

Every day, I...

remind myself that I am response-able, and I assume full and entire responsibility for my day ahead. I create the outcome of my life. No one else does it for me. I am in charge, I am in control.

<u>Blessings</u> I start by putting on my French Amour™ silver ring and reminding myself of five blessings that have been bestowed upon me:

1) ....
....
2) ....
....
3) ....
....
4) ....
....
5) ....
....

<u>Self-Improvement</u> Today I will focus on...

....
....
....
....
....
....
....

<u>Self-Appreciation</u> Today I will appreciate my mind, body, and soul through the following activities:

Mind:

Body:

Soul:

<u>Forgiveness</u> As I remove my ring for the night, I forgive anyone who hurt me, intentionally or by accident. I forgive myself for any perceived shortcomings, as I know I've tried my best.

I forgive:

<u>Journaling</u> Tell me more about the feelings and emotions you've experienced throughout your day. What did you do today to take one step further toward achieving your goal and/or improving the area that needs your attention?

Love-Lock It 🔒

Love is only one aspect of a long, loving relationship.

Copy this statement. Write it, so you remember it in mind, body, and soul.

....
....

Day 12.

Date: ....

Every day, I ....

remind myself that I am response-able, and I assume full and entire responsibility for my day ahead. I create the outcome of my life. No one else does it for me. I am in charge, I am in control.

<u>Blessings</u> I start by putting on my French Amour™ silver ring and reminding myself of five blessings that have been bestowed upon me:

1) ....
....
2) ....
....
3) ....
....
4) ....
....
5) ....
....

<u>Self-Improvement</u> Today I will focus on...

....
....
....
....
....
....
....

<u>Self-Appreciation</u> Today I will appreciate my mind, body, and soul through the following activities:

Mind: ....
....

Body: ....
....

Soul: ....
....

<u>Forgiveness</u> As I remove my ring for the night, I forgive anyone who hurt me, intentionally or by accident. I forgive myself for any perceived shortcomings, as I know I've tried my best.

I forgive:

Journaling Tell me more about the feelings and emotions you've experienced throughout your day. What did you do today to take one step further toward achieving your goal and/or improving the area that needs your attention?

Love-Lock It 🔒

Disagreements and arguments do not mean we are incompatible.

Copy this statement. Write it, so you remember it in mind, body, and soul. ✎

....
....

Day 13.

Date: ....

Every day, I ....

remind myself that I am response-able, and I assume full and entire responsibility for my day ahead. I create the outcome of my life. No one else does it for me. I am in charge, I am in control.

<u>Blessings</u> I start by putting on my French Amour™ silver ring and reminding myself of five blessings that have been bestowed upon me:

1) ....
....
2) ....
....
3) ....
....
4) ....
....
5) ....
....

<u>Self-Improvement</u> Today I will focus on...

....
....
....
....
....
....
....

<u>Self-Appreciation</u> Today I will appreciate my mind, body, and soul through the following activities:

Mind:..
....

Body:..
....

Soul:..
....

<u>Forgiveness</u> As I remove my ring for the night, I forgive anyone who hurt me, intentionally or by accident. I forgive myself for any perceived shortcomings, as I know I've tried my best.

I forgive:

__Journaling__ Tell me more about the feelings and emotions you've experienced throughout your day. What did you do today to take one step further toward achieving your goal and/or improving the area that needs your attention?

Love-Lock It 🔒

Chemistry is stronger than algorithms.

Copy this statement. Write it, so you remember it in mind, body, and soul. ✍

....

....

Day 14.

Date: ....

Every day, I ....

remind myself that I am response-able, and I assume full and entire responsibility for my day ahead. I create the outcome of my life. No one else does it for me. I am in charge, I am in control.

<u>Blessings</u> I start by putting on my French Amour™ silver ring and reminding myself of five blessings that have been bestowed upon me:

1) ....

2) ....

3) ....

4) ....

5) ....

<u>Self-Improvement</u> Today I will focus on...

<u>Self-Appreciation</u> Today I will appreciate my mind, body, and soul through the following activities:

Mind: ....

....

Body: ....

....

Soul: ....

....

<u>Forgiveness</u> As I remove my ring for the night, I forgive anyone who hurt me, intentionally or by accident. I forgive myself for any perceived shortcomings, as I know I've tried my best.

I forgive:

<u>Journaling</u> Tell me more about the feelings and emotions you've experienced throughout your day. What did you do today to take one step further toward achieving your goal and/or improving the area that needs your attention?

Love-Lock It 🔒

I don't need to be "perfect"—and neither does my future partner.

Copy this statement. Write it, so you remember it in mind, body, and soul. ✎

....
....

Day 15.

Date: ....

Every day, I ....

remind myself that I am response-able, and I assume full and entire responsibility for my day ahead. I create the outcome of my life. No one else does it for me. I am in charge, I am in control.

<u>Blessings</u> I start by putting on my French Amour™ silver ring and reminding myself of five blessings that have been bestowed upon me:

1) ....
....
2) ....
....
3) ....
....
4) ....
....
5) ....
....

<u>Self-Improvement</u> Today I will focus on...

....
....
....
....
....
....
....

<u>Self-Appreciation</u> Today I will appreciate my mind, body, and soul through the following activities:

Mind: ....

Body: ....

Soul: ....

<u>Forgiveness</u> As I remove my ring for the night, I forgive anyone who hurt me, intentionally or by accident. I forgive myself for any perceived shortcomings, as I know I've tried my best.

I forgive:

__Journaling__ Tell me more about the feelings and emotions you've experienced throughout your day. What did you do today to take one step further toward achieving your goal and/or improving the area that needs your attention?

Love-Lock It 🔒

There really are plenty of fish in the sea. My partner and I will find each other.

Copy this statement. Write it, so you remember it in mind, body, and soul. ✍

....

....

Day 16.

Date: ....

Every day, I ....

remind myself that I am response-able, and I assume full and entire responsibility for my day ahead. I create the outcome of my life. No one else does it for me. I am in charge, I am in control.

Blessings I start by putting on my French Amour™ silver ring and reminding myself of five blessings that have been bestowed upon me:

1) ....
....
2) ....
....
3) ....
....
4) ....
....
5) ....
....

Self-Improvement Today I will focus on...

....
....
....
....
....
....
....

<u>Self-Appreciation</u> Today I will appreciate my mind, body, and soul through the following activities:

Mind: ....
....

Body: ....
....

Soul: ....
....

<u>Forgiveness</u> As I remove my ring for the night, I forgive anyone who hurt me, intentionally or by accident. I forgive myself for any perceived shortcomings, as I know I've tried my best.

I forgive:

<u>Journaling</u> Tell me more about the feelings and emotions you've experienced throughout your day. What did you do today to take one step further toward achieving your goal and/or improving the area that needs your attention?

Love-Lock It 🔒

My S.M.A.R.T goals are mine, and they are good for me.

Copy this statement. Write it, so you remember it in mind, body, and soul. ✍

....
....

Day 17.

Date: ....

Every day, I..

remind myself that I am response-able, and I assume full and entire responsibility for my day ahead. I create the outcome of my life. No one else does it for me. I am in charge, I am in control.

<u>Blessings</u> I start by putting on my French Amour™ silver ring and reminding myself of five blessings that have been bestowed upon me:

1) ....
....
2) ....
....
3) ....
....
4) ....
....
5) ....
....

<u>Self-Improvement</u> Today I will focus on...

....
....
....
....
....
....
....

<u>Self-Appreciation</u> Today I will appreciate my mind, body, and soul through the following activities:

Mind: ....
....
Body: ....
....
Soul: ....
....

<u>Forgiveness</u> As I remove my ring for the night, I forgive anyone who hurt me, intentionally or by accident. I forgive myself for any perceived shortcomings, as I know I've tried my best.

I forgive:

<u>Journaling</u> Tell me more about the feelings and emotions you've experienced throughout your day. What did you do today to take one step further toward achieving your goal and/or improving the area that needs your attention?

Love-Lock It 🔒

Cupid is not real. Reason, honesty, and effort will help me find my soulmate.

Copy this statement. Write it, so you remember it in mind, body, and soul.

....
....

Day 18.

Date: ....

Every day, I ....

remind myself that I am response-able, and I assume full and entire responsibility for my day ahead. I create the outcome of my life. No one else does it for me. I am in charge, I am in control.

<u>Blessings</u> I start by putting on my French Amour™ silver ring and reminding myself of five blessings that have been bestowed upon me:

1) ....
....
2) ....
....
3) ....
....
4) ....
....
5) ....
....

<u>Self-Improvement</u> Today I will focus on...

<u>Self-Appreciation</u> Today I will appreciate my mind, body, and soul through the following activities:

Mind: ....

Body: ....

Soul: ....

<u>Forgiveness</u> As I remove my ring for the night, I forgive anyone who hurt me, intentionally or by accident. I forgive myself for any perceived shortcomings, as I know I've tried my best.

I forgive:

__Journaling__ Tell me more about the feelings and emotions you've experienced throughout your day. What did you do today to take one step further toward achieving your goal and/or improving the area that needs your attention?

Love-Lock It 🔒

Grace is an integral part of a good relationship.

Copy this statement. Write it, so you remember it in mind, body, and soul. ✍

....
....

Day 19.

Date: ....

Every day, I ....

remind myself that I am response-able, and I assume full and entire responsibility for my day ahead. I create the outcome of my life. No one else does it for me. I am in charge, I am in control.

<u>Blessings</u> I start by putting on my French Amour™ silver ring and reminding myself of five blessings that have been bestowed upon me:

1) ....
....
2) ....
....
3) ....
....
4) ....
....
5) ....
....

<u>Self-Improvement</u> Today I will focus on...

....
....
....
....
....
....
....

<u>Self-Appreciation</u> Today I will appreciate my mind, body, and soul through the following activities:

Mind: ....
....

Body: ....
....

Soul: ....
....

<u>Forgiveness</u> As I remove my ring for the night, I forgive anyone who hurt me, intentionally or by accident. I forgive myself for any perceived shortcomings, as I know I've tried my best.

I forgive:

Journaling Tell me more about the feelings and emotions you've experienced throughout your day. What did you do today to take one step further toward achieving your goal and/or improving the area that needs your attention?

Love-Lock It 🔒

Presence is essential for love.

Copy this statement. Write it, so you remember it in mind, body, and soul. ✍

....

....

Day 20.

Date: ....

Every day, I..

remind myself that I am response-able, and I assume full and entire responsibility for my day ahead. I create the outcome of my life. No one else does it for me. I am in charge, I am in control.

<u>Blessings</u> I start by putting on my French Amour™ silver ring and reminding myself of five blessings that have been bestowed upon me:

1) ....
....
2) ....
....
3) ....
....
4) ....
....
5) ....
....

<u>Self-Improvement</u> Today I will focus on...

....
....
....
....
....
....
....

<u>Self-Appreciation</u> Today I will appreciate my mind, body, and soul through the following activities:

Mind:

Body:

Soul:

<u>Forgiveness</u> As I remove my ring for the night, I forgive anyone who hurt me, intentionally or by accident. I forgive myself for any perceived shortcomings, as I know I've tried my best.

I forgive:

Journaling Tell me more about the feelings and emotions you've experienced throughout your day. What did you do today to take one step further toward achieving your goal and/or improving the area that needs your attention?

Love-Lock It 🔒

When we fall for each other, we will be ready to catch each other.

Copy this statement. Write it, so you remember it in mind, body, and soul. ✍

....
....

Day 21.

Date: ....

Every day, I ....

remind myself that I am response-able, and I assume full and entire responsibility for my day ahead. I create the outcome of my life. No one else does it for me. I am in charge, I am in control.

<u>Blessings</u> I start by putting on my French Amour™ silver ring and reminding myself of five blessings that have been bestowed upon me:

1) ....
....
2) ....
....
3) ....
....
4) ....
....
5) ....
....

<u>Self-Improvement</u> Today I will focus on...

....
....
....
....
....
....
....

<u>Self-Appreciation</u> Today I will appreciate my mind, body, and soul through the following activities:

Mind: ....

Body: ....

Soul: ....

<u>Forgiveness</u> As I remove my ring for the night, I forgive anyone who hurt me, intentionally or by accident. I forgive myself for any perceived shortcomings, as I know I've tried my best.

I forgive:

Journaling Tell me more about the feelings and emotions you've experienced throughout your day. What did you do today to take one step further toward achieving your goal and/or improving the area that needs your attention?

Congratulations! You've finished your 21 days of journaling!

I'm sure you've learned a ton about yourself, the amazing person you want to be and, most importantly, the fantastic partner you want to meet in a very near future.

DO NOT SETTLE FOR ANYONE!

DO NOT SEEK THE COMFORTABLE PATTERNS.

You just spent 21 days working on yourself, loving yourself like never before.

Your life plan and what you seek on online dating sites should be different now. I strongly recommend you take it slowly. Do not seek the immediate gratification of the first date. Take your time.

If you need company, you have friends. If you seek sexual pleasure, you have yourself and access to your toys.

Do not jump head first into that pool anymore. Caution, respect, and loving yourself are the most important aspects of next loving relationship.

Now, it's time to meet your dream-come-true.

Remember that your date should reflect your love for yourself. It should be intimate and leave you space to communicate openly with yourself. It should reflect your goals and values for your future relationship.

Parisian Date: Preparation

Get ready for your date.

Preparation makes you feel calm and collected. It also demonstrates your interest in and commitment to the activity.

What do you do to get ready?

Preparing my Body

These are the things I am doing to prepare my body before my date:

....
....
....
....
....
....
....
....
....
....
....
....

Until you have worked through the stages and are prepared to commit to physical intimacy, I suggest you release your sexual energy before each date (even before this date with yourself). Implement the activity as part of your body preparation. This way, you will be calm, composed, and focused on the conversation—not distracted by the thought of the "after dinner activity". On average, it can take 5 dates before you know someone well enough to commit to physical intimacy: do not offer your temple of love to anyone who is not willing to work through the stages of intimacy with you. You will always have yourself. Respect and appreciate your own body.

Dressing

My clothes are comfortable, make me feel attractive, and communicate my personality and values. This is what I am wearing on my Parisian date:

....
....
....
....
....
....

Ornamentation

Decoration is the icing on the cake. This is how I'll do any make-up I feel comfortable wearing, and the jewelry I'll use to accessorize:

....
....
....
....
....
....

Love-Lock It 🔒

I am beautiful, inside and out.

Copy this statement. Write it, so you remember it in mind, body, and soul. ✐

....
....

Preparing My Mind

The mind needs to be calm and collected before heading into a new situation. These are the things I am doing to prepare my mind before my date.

....
....
....
....
....
....
....
....
....
....
....
....
....
....
....
....
....

Now, you're ready for your Parisian date. How are you feeling?

Tell me more.

Your Parisian Date: Dinner

This is where I would like to go to eat:

I would like to go there because...

This is what I would like to eat:

I would like to eat this because...

Love-Lock It 🔒

My preferences reflect who I am.

Copy this statement. Write it, so you remember it in mind, body, and soul. ✐

....
....

These are the topics I would like to discuss during dinner:

....
....
....

I would like to discuss these things because...

....
....
....
....
....
....
....
....
....
....
....

Life is a matter of choices,

and every choice you make makes you you!

- John C. Maxwell

Your Parisian Date: After Dinner

This is where I would like to go after we have eaten:

....
....
....

I would like to go there because...

....
....
....
....
....
....
....
....
....
....
....

This is what I would like to see while we are there:

....
....
....

I would like to see this because...

....
....
....
....

These are the topics I would like to discuss after dinner:

....
....
....

I would like to discuss these things because...

....
....
....
....
....
....
....
....
....

Your Parisian Date: The Ultimate Conclusion

This is the perfect ending to the date:

It is the perfect ending because...

We cannot start over, but we can begin now, and make a new beginning.

- Zig Ziglar

This perfect Parisian date supports my goals and values in these ways:

🔒 It demonstrates my self-responsibility in this way:

....
....
....

🔒 It demonstrates self-love in this way:

....
....
....

🔒 It demonstrates self-affirmation in this way:

....
....
....

🔒 It demonstrates self-improvement in this way:

....
....
....

🔒 It demonstrates self-forgiveness in this way:

....
....
....

🔒 It demonstrates self-appreciation in this way:

....
....
....

🔒 It relates to intimacy in this way:

....
....
....

🔒 It demonstrates emotional intimacy in this way:

....
....
....

🔒 It demonstrates spiritual intimacy in this way:

....
....
....

🔒 It demonstrates physical intimacy in this way:

....
....
....

🔒 It relates to communication in this way:

....
....
....

🔒 It relates to common goals and values in this way.

....
....
....

Are there any aspects of the date that you need to change so they support the growth you've accomplished over the last 21 days?

....
....
....
....
....
....
....
....
....
....
....
....
....
....
....

Now that you've planned your perfect Parisian date, I want you to go on that date. Don't fret: if you can't afford a trip to Paris, a local equivalent will do just fine.

If you are not yet ready to be with a romantic partner, then take yourself.

Dress for yourself.

Dine alone.

Walk alone.

Look at the stars alone.

Get to know yourself as intimately as possible.

What you *should* take with you is this journal. Whenever you notice something or feel something, write it down. Don't be afraid of it. This is the real, perfect you.

....
....
....
....
....
....
....
....
....

Conclusion

My Dear Journaler...

This journal is my personal gift to you.

🔒 You are the perfect you. You deserve to find your soulmate and live the life you want to lead. What has happened so far in your life is in the past. This is **now**, your present, your reality. Your future is clean and bright.

🔒 You are response-ABLE. You have accepted responsibility for your own life, for the things you say and do, for your reactions to everything that happens around you. All the tools and skills you need are within you. You are not a victim: you are in control, and you are strong.

🔒 Now that you are aware of your self-love, you can communicate it to others. You have clarified who you are and what you want, and you have accepted that you are the *perfect* you—no need to lie on profiles, no need to compromise on your values, and no need to give without receiving.

🔒 You have improved your intimacy with yourself. You know how you feel, what you believe in, what your body needs. You are beautifully close with yourself, and you can be close with others. The intimate bonds you create will be as flexible and unbreakable as silk.

🔒 You have improved your communication with yourself. By listening to your heart and soul, you've connected with who you truly are, and you have learned that you need to listen to that wise and kind inner voice. You have also improved your communication with others: you can hear what they're saying, respond well, and use the communication effectively to move your relationship forward.

🔒 You have clearly established your goals and values. You know you need to find a partner who shares these goals and values, or at least has goals and values that don't clash with yours. You and your new partner will both be facing in the same direction and walking the same path towards the same destination.

🔒 All this new information helps you break the chains of old relationship patterns, setting you free to explore love in a bright, healthy manner.

You've put a *lot* of work into this. Now that you've made all this effort, you're no longer wasting time.

Go back on your dating site(s). Take your profile off "pause". Improve the profile so it shows the REAL you.

You are have nothing to hide. People will be pleasantly surprised to interact with someone who has so much self-confidence and knows exactly what they want out of a relationship. The people who connect with you will want to know more about your life philosophy.

Communicate that philosophy through your profile.

When you look at other people, look for profiles where the prospective partner has obviously communicated as well as you have. Feel their self-love in their profile. See if they respect intimacy the way you do. Make note of their communication skills. Look for your shared values and goals.

Your new philosophy is simple; however, any simple principle holds a fundamental truth that requires dedication and determination. Living by the Four Secrets mentioned in this book will transform lives around you. You've started with your own!

The power that you have acquired with this new knowledge is immense.

As a hundred single drops of water will eventually fill a glass, every step you take towards love and happiness will improve your life. These steps you've taken are an excellent beginning to filling your life with the relationships you want.

Though you've reached the end of this journal, do not stop making an effort! As I recommended earlier, come back to this book and rate the statements again. Make note of what has changed and what has remained the same; make note of what has turned out well and what you still need to work on. Life is constant. Like any other organic creature, if you do not renew yourself on a regular basis, you will stagnate and rot. Surviving is not thriving!

As well, continue to journal daily. Remember to be grateful for your five daily blessings, love yourself, be intimate, communicate properly, and remain clear about your values and goals. You've earned your secret rings: use them, and be proud of them!

When you find yourself able to trust a person—a lover or a close friend—feel free to share parts of this journal with them. This will open more channels of communication and give you the opportunity to discuss values and goals. You may find you've been unintentionally hiding aspects of yourself that others find attractive and interesting.

You will not run out of time, now. You will not subject yourself to the ravages of loneliness.

You will find love.

If you haven't already, I recommend you read *The Four Secret Rings of Love and Happiness*. Let Émilie's journey with her family, friends, and lovers inspire you to take your journey even further.

Join our private Facebook *group*
French Amour Elite Club

Our Elite Club comes with great privileges.

Not only will you be joining like-minded friends who focus on love and happiness, but you will benefit from amazing savings on our upcoming products.

www.ingramcontent.com/pod-product-compliance
Lightning Source LLC
LaVergne TN
LVHW041611070426
835507LV00008B/192